Kakapo Coloring Book For Adults

Birds Coloring Book for Adults Relaxation containing 20 Paisley, Henna and Mandala Coloring Pages

Birds Coloring Books for Grown-Ups: Vol 1

by The Coloring Book People

Copyright © 2017 by The Coloring Book People
All rights reserved. No part of this publication may be reproduced, distributed, or transmitted in any form or by any means, including photocopying, recording, or other electronic or mechanical methods, without the prior written permission of the publisher.

ISBN-13: 978-1544287584

ISBN-10: 1544287585

Preview

.

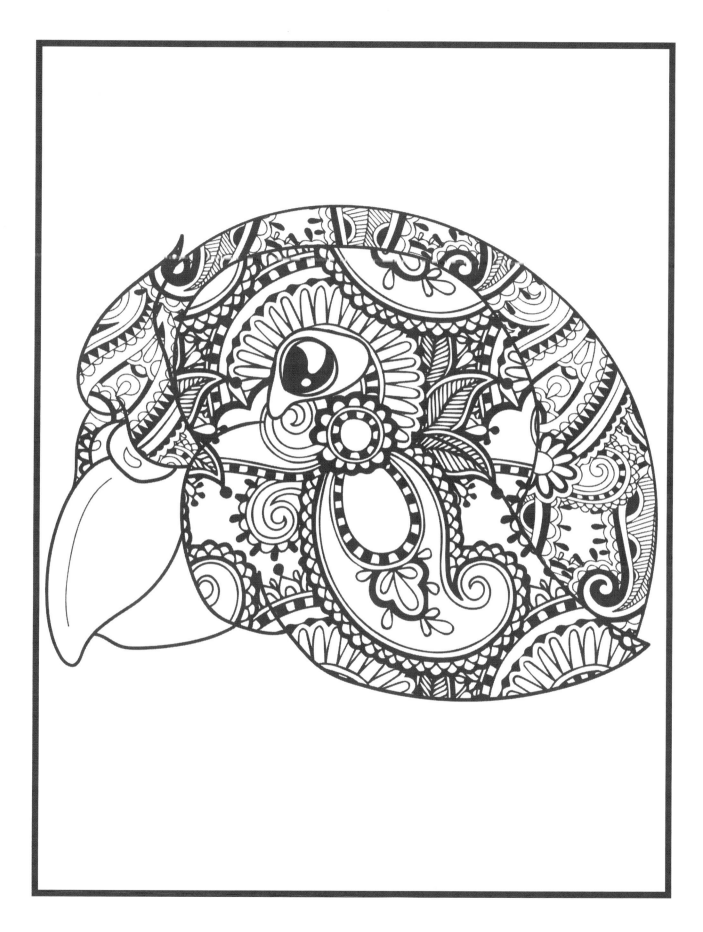

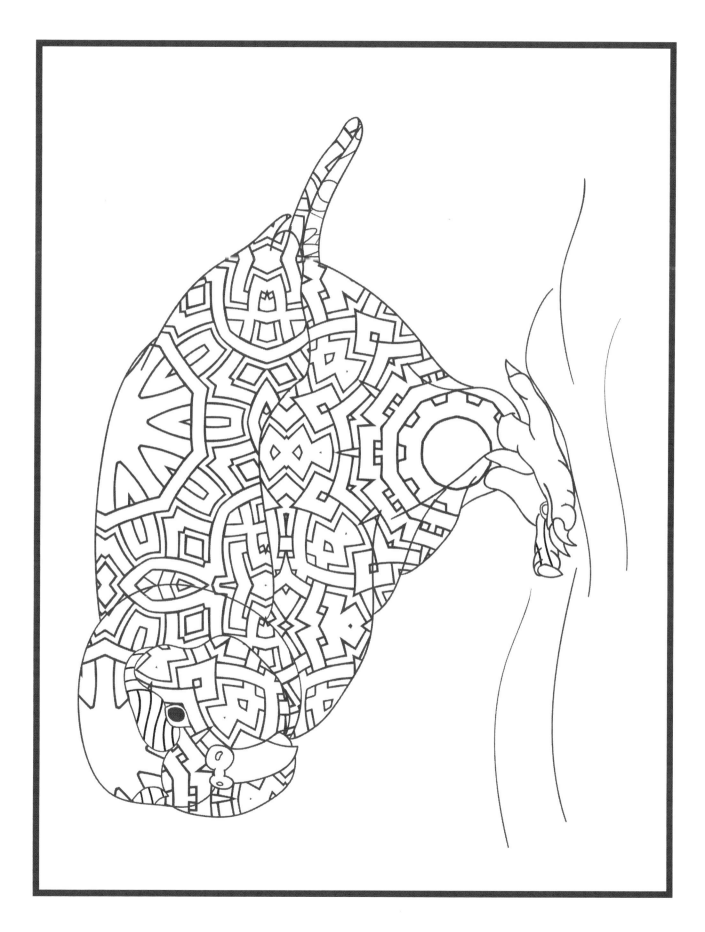

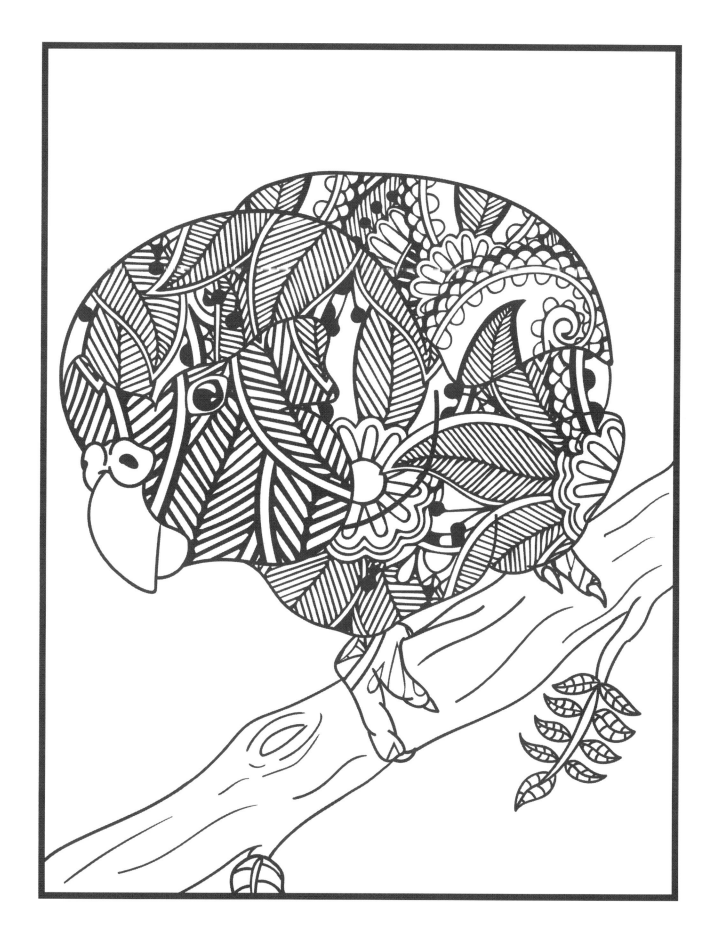

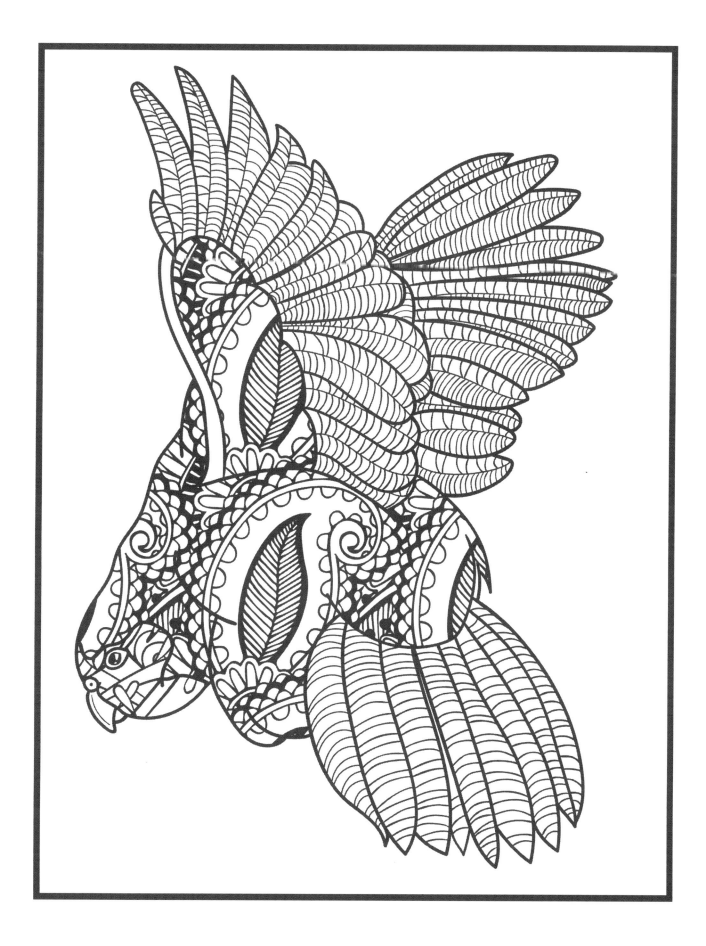

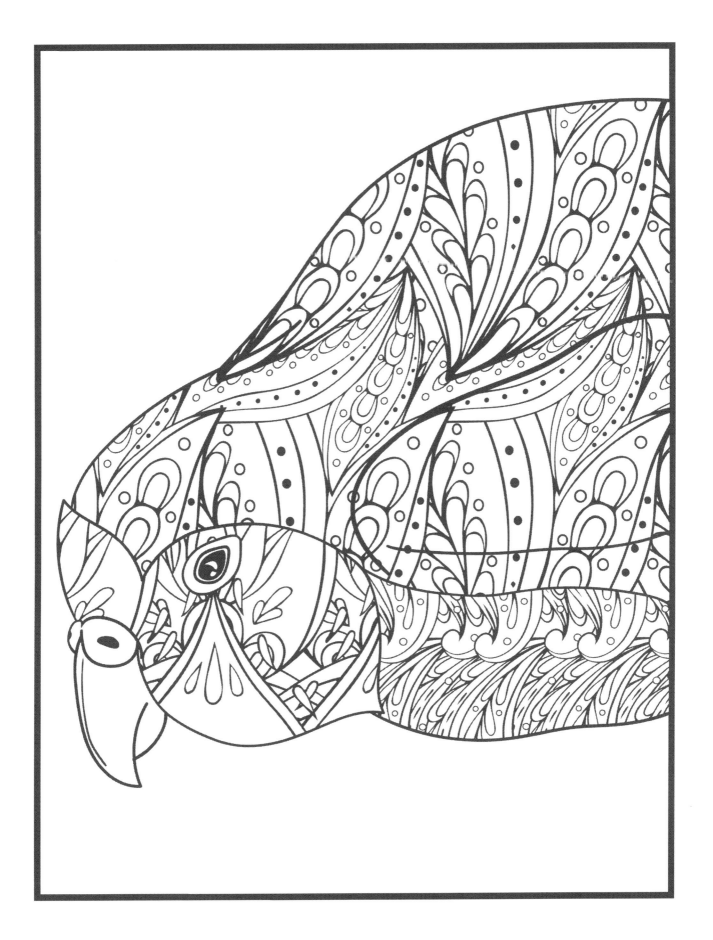

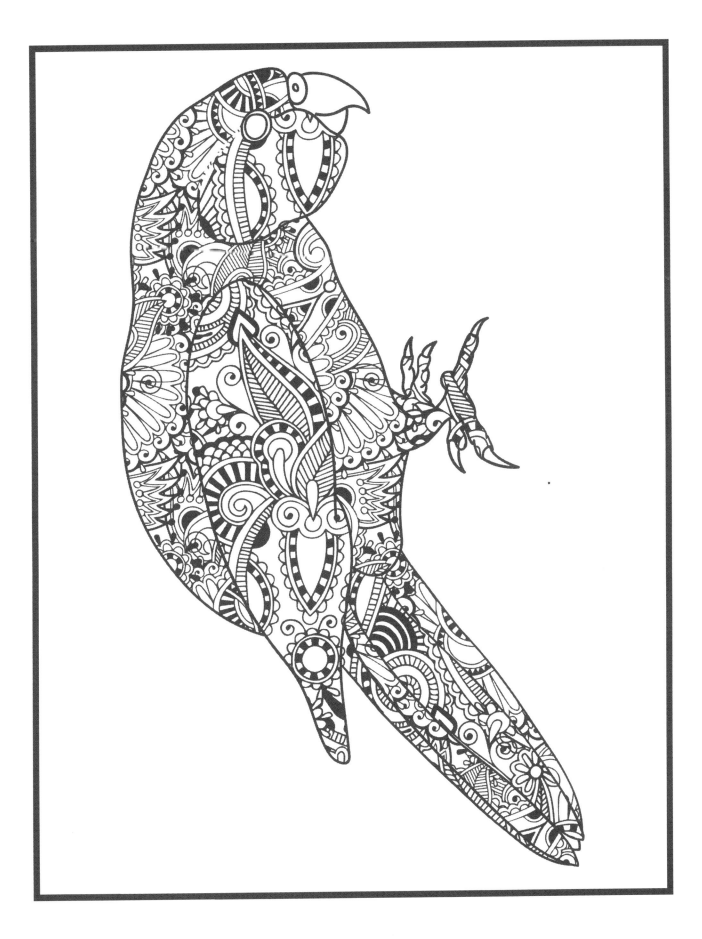

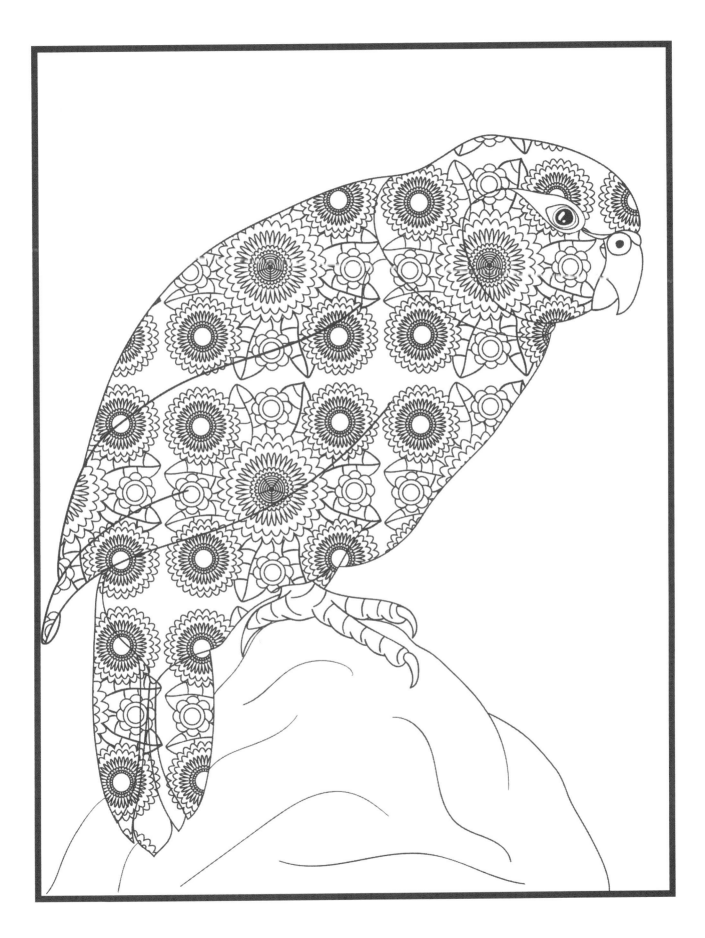

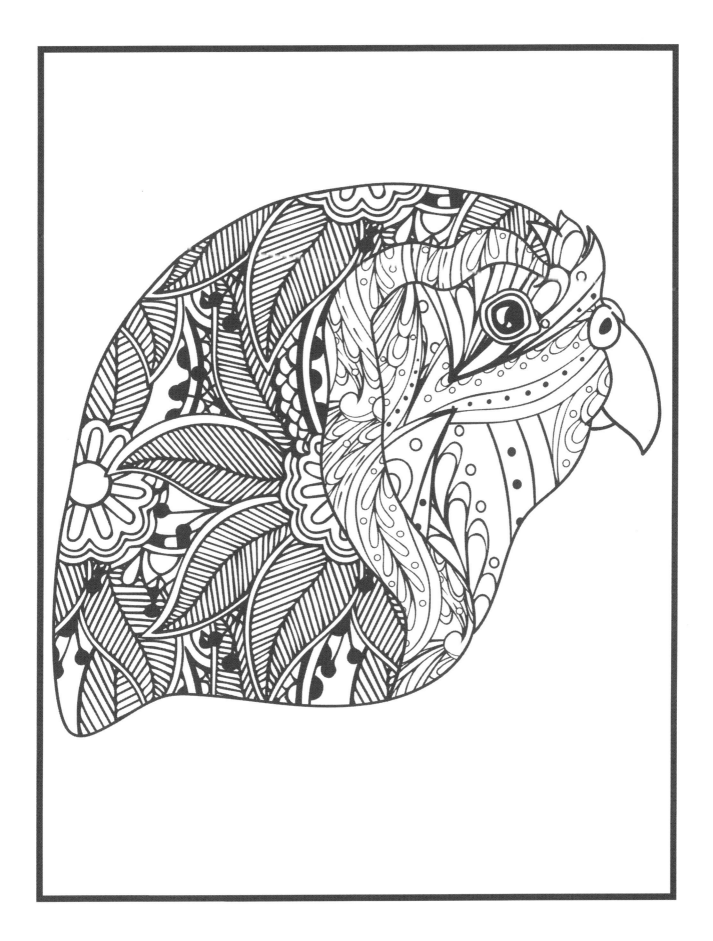

COLOR TEST PAGE

COLOR TEST PAGE

Made in the USA
San Bernardino, CA
10 September 2018